Musty–Crusty
Animals

Sea Horses

Lola M. Schaefer

Heinemann Library
Chicago, Illinois

Customer Service 888-454-2279
Visit our website at www.heinemannlibrary.com

Designed by Sue Emerson/Heinemann Library and Ginkgo Creative, Inc.
Printed and bound in China by South China Printing Company

06
10 9 8

Library of Congress Cataloging-in-Publication Data
Schaefer, Lola M., 1950-
    Sea horses / Lola Schaefer.
        p. cm. — (Musty-crusty animals)
Includes index.
Summary: A basic introduction to sea horses, discussing their physical characteristics, habitat, diet, and activities.
    ISBN 1-58810-517-2 (lib. bdg.)   ISBN 1-58810-726-4 (pbk. bdg.)
    1. Sea horses—Juvenile literature. [1. Sea horses.] I. Title.
    QL638.S9 S34 2002
    597'.6798—dc21

                            2001003286

Acknowledgments
The author and publishers are grateful to the following for permission to reproduce copyright material:
Title page, p. 16 David Liebman; pp. 4, 17, 22 E. R. Degginger/Color Pic, Inc.; pp. 5, 10, 12, 15L Edward G. Lines, Jr./John G. Shedd Aquarium; p. 6 Jeff Rotman Photography; p. 7 Paul Humann/Jeff Rotman Photography; p. 8 Dan Burton/Seapics.com; p. 9 Doug Perrine/Seapics.com; p. 11 John G. Shedd Aquarium/Visuals Unlimited; p. 13 Patrice Ceisel/Visuals Unlimited; pp. 14, 20, 21 Rudie Kuiter/Seapics.com; p. 15R Alex Kerstitch/Visuals Unlimited; p. 18 Brandon D. Cole; p. 19 David Kearnes/Seapics.com; glossary (vertebrate) Dennis Sheridan

Cover photograph courtesy of Eda Rogers

Every effort has been made to contact copyright holders of any material reproduced in this book. Any omissions will be rectified in subsequent printings if notice is given to the publisher.

Special thanks to our advisory panel for their help in the preparation of this book:
Eileen Day, Preschool Teacher
Chicago, IL

Paula Fischer, K–1 Teacher
Indianapolis, IN

Sandra Gilbert, Library
Media Specialist
Houston, TX

Angela Leeper,
Educational Consultant
North Carolina Department
of Public Instruction
Raleigh, NC

Pam McDonald,
Reading Teacher
Winter Springs, FL

Melinda Murphy,
Library Media Specialist
Houston, TX

Helen Rosenberg, MLS
Chicago, IL

Anna Marie Varakin,
Reading Instructor
Western Maryland College

Special thanks to Dr. Randy Kochevar of the Monterey Bay Aquarium for his help in the preparation of this book.

Some words are shown in bold, **like this.**
You can find them in the picture glossary on page 23.

Contents

What Are Sea Horses?

Sea horses are animals with bones.

They are **vertebrates**.

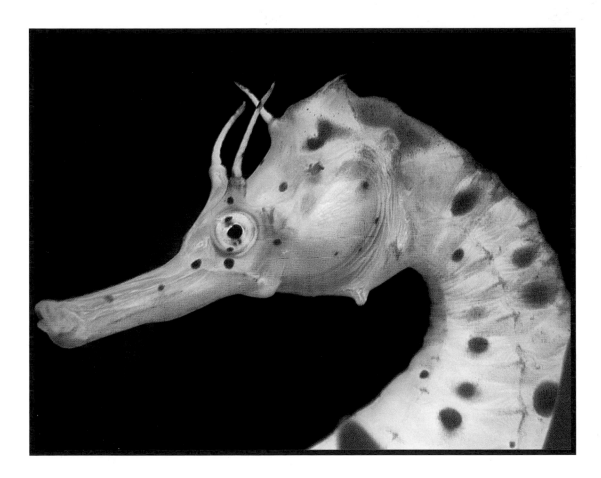

Sea horses are small fish.

They are not horses at all.

Where Do Sea Horses Live?

Sea horses live in the ocean.

They live in warm water near land.

coral

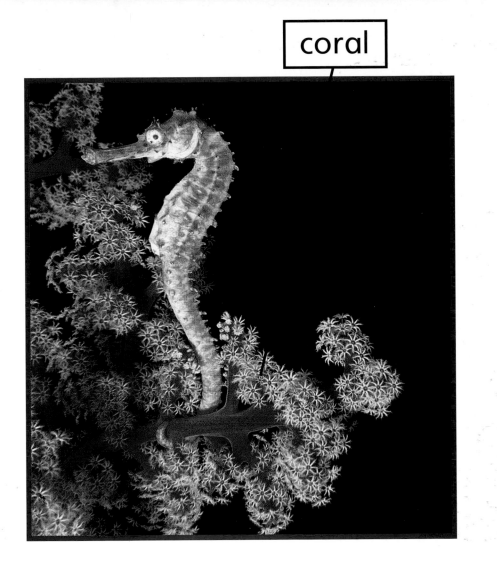

Most sea horses live near sea plants or **coral**.

What Do Sea Horses Look Like?

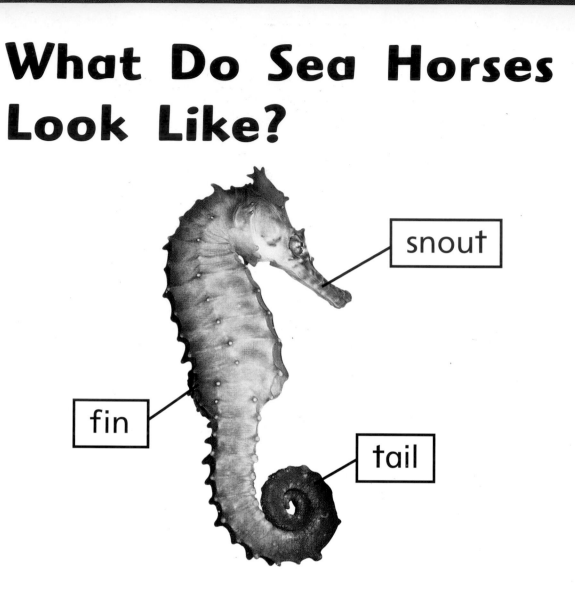

snout

fin

tail

Sea horses have long **snouts** and curled tails.

Fins help them swim.

eye

Sea horses have two large eyes.

Some sea horses look like little dragons!

Do Sea Horses Have Shells?

Sea horses do not have shells.

They have rings of bony parts inside their bodies.

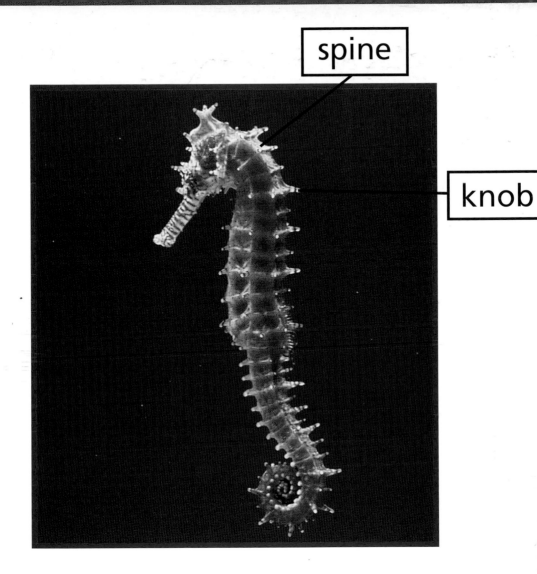

spine

knob

Sea horses have **knobs** and **spines.**

These keep them safe from
other fish.

What Do Sea Horses Feel Like?

Sea horses feel wet.

Their bodies feel bony through the skin.

spine

Many sea horses feel prickly.

Their **spines** can be sharp.

How Big Are Sea Horses?

Young sea horses are the length of an eyelash.

Adult sea horses can be many sizes.

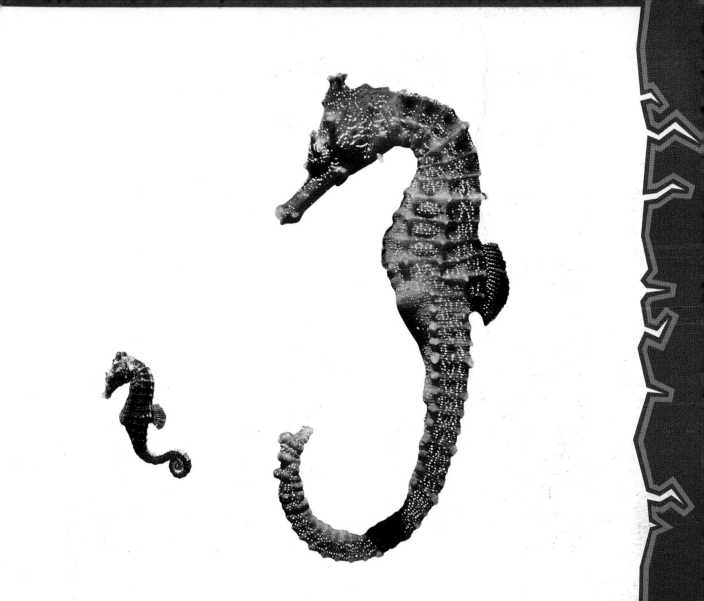

The smallest sea horse is the size of an ant.

The largest sea horse is as long as two pencils.

How Do Sea Horses Move?

fin

Sea horses swim.

They swim by moving their **fins** back and forth.

Big waves can carry sea horses from place to place.

What Do Sea Horses Eat?

Sea horses eat shrimp and **plankton**.

Plankton are tiny animals that float in sea water.

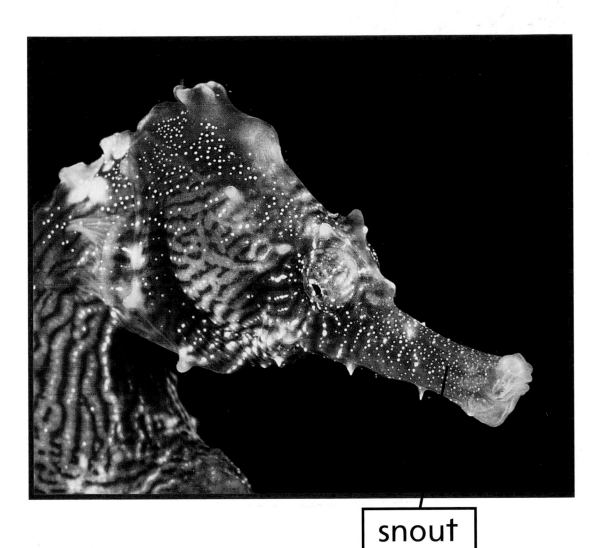

snout

Sea horses suck food out of the water with their **snouts**.

Where Do New Sea Horses Come From?

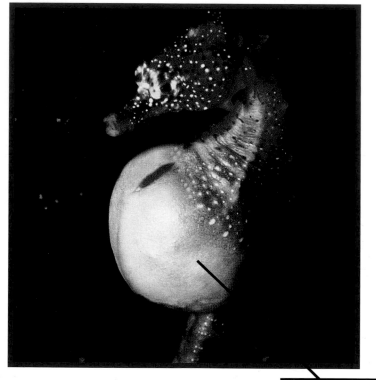

pouch

Female sea horses lay eggs.

They lay them in the **pouch** of the male sea horse.

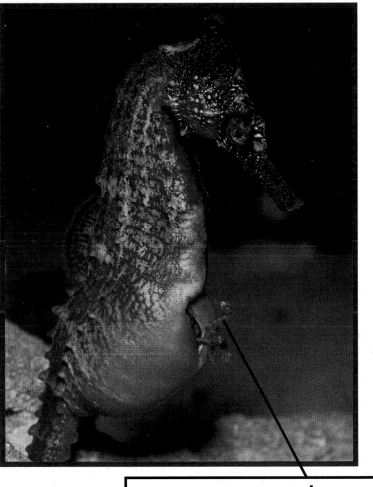

young sea horse

The eggs hatch.

Young sea horses pop out into the ocean.

Quiz

What are these sea horse parts?

Can you find them in the book?

Look for the answers on page 24.

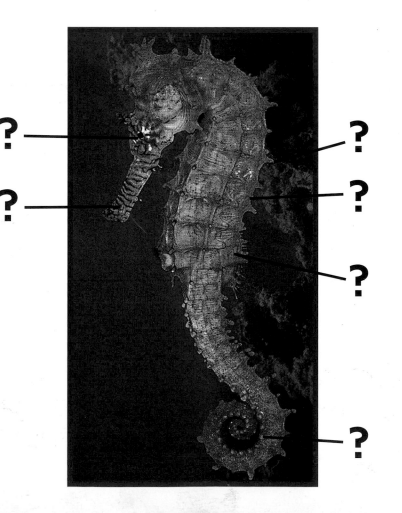

Picture Glossary

coral
page 7

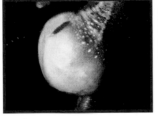
pouch
page 20

fin
pages 8, 16

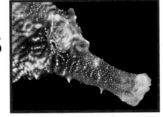
snout
pages 8, 19

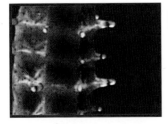
knobs
page 11

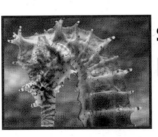
spines
pages 11, 13

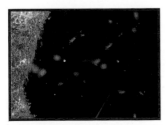
plankton
page 18

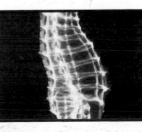
vertebrate
(VUR-tuh-brate)
page 4

Note to Parents and Teachers

Reading for information is an important part of a child's literacy development. Learning begins with a question about something. Help children think of themselves as investigators and researchers by encouraging their questions about the world around them. Each chapter in this book begins with a question. Read the question together. Look at the pictures. Talk about what you think the answer might be. Then read the text to find out if your predictions were correct. Think of other questions you could ask about the topic, and discuss where you might find the answers. Assist children in using the picture glossary and the index to practice new vocabulary and research skills.

! CAUTION: Remind children that it is not a good idea to handle wild animals. Children should wash their hands with soap and water after they touch any animal.

Index

Answers to quiz on page 22

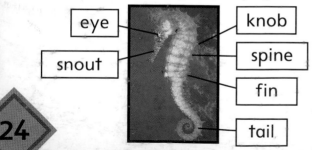

eye
snout
knob
spine
fin
tail